7

COUPLES CONVERSATIONS

TO STRENGTHEN YOUR RELATIONSHIP FOR GOOD

Iona Yeung
30everafter

HOW TO USE
THIS BOOK

Navigate through tricky conversations that may be hard to approach. Think of it as a guide to help you and your partner find middle ground on challenging topics.

You'll find that you may not always agree but with some patience and love, I hope you both will find a way to foster a stronger relationship.

Choose a topic that you both want to discuss and stick to one topic per conversation.

RULES OF ENGAGEMENT

 RULE # 1: ASK QUESTIONS.

 RULE # 2: TRY YOUR BEST.

 RULE # 3: BE HONEST.

 RULE # 4: LISTEN.

 RULE # 5: BE RESPECTFUL.

THE MONEY TALK

CREATING WEALTH TOGETHER

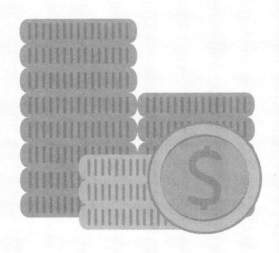

Name:	Year:	Date:	Partner A:

YOUR MONEY STORY

Your money story says a lot about how you grew up learning and thinking about money. This drives a lot of the decisions you now make.

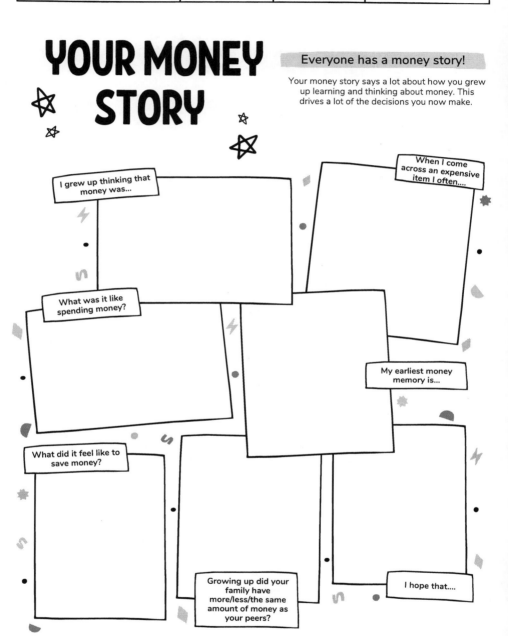

I grew up thinking that money was...

When I come across an expensive item I often....

What was it like spending money?

My earliest money memory is...

What did it feel like to save money?

Growing up did your family have more/less/the same amount of money as your peers?

I hope that....

Name:	Year:	Date:	Partner B:

YOUR MONEY STORY

Everyone has a money story!

Your money story says a lot about how you grew up learning and thinking about money. This drives a lot of the decisions you now make.

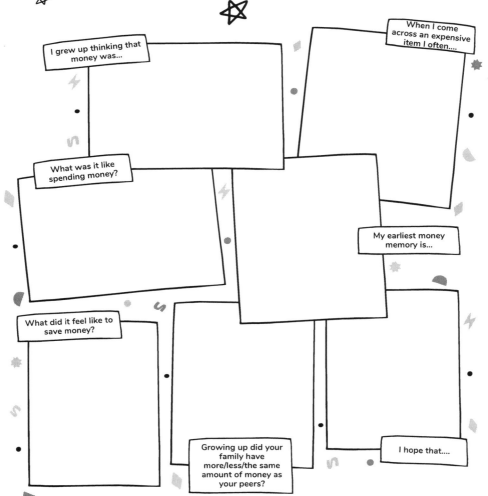

I grew up thinking that money was...

When I come across an expensive item I often....

What was it like spending money?

My earliest money memory is...

What did it feel like to save money?

Growing up did your family have more/less/the same amount of money as your peers?

I hope that....

THE MONEY TALK
Your Money Beliefs

Money is the root of most conflict in a relationship. We adopt our money habits from a very young age. We witness our parents speak and manage their finances and this has an effect on our money beliefs. You might have one partner who grew up in an environment where money was scarce and another who was taught how to use money to generate more money.

A conflict in money beliefs can lead to many heated conversations about how you manage finances as a household. Use these prompts to start the conversation. Remember, the topic of money is charged with emotions. Be patient and take the time to understand your partner.

MONEY BELIEFS

1. Fill in the blank. To me, money is _____.?

2. How much is a lot of money to you?

3. What is a comfortable amount of money to have in the bank?

GROWING UP WITH MONEY

1. How would you describe your parents' relationship with money?

2. Were your parents spenders or savers?

3. Who managed the finances in your household?

NOTES

_____   _____

_____   _____

_____   _____

_____   _____

THE MONEY TALK
Sharing the details

How much do you share about your finances?
Is it taboo to talk about it? Find out with a discussion.

TALKING ABOUT MONEY

1. Do you share how much you earn?

2. Do you believe your financial affairs should be kept private?

3. If your friend or family member asked to borrow money, would you say yes?

MANAGING MONEY AS A COUPLE

1. How do you feel about joining our finances?

2. How would you like to manage money as a couple? i.e. Joint savings and spending account?

3. If one of us earns significantly more than the other, how much should we each allocate to a join savings account?

 Tip: If one person earns more than the other, each should allocate a percentage of their salary to the joint savings account.

THE MONEY TALK
Working with a Budget

Planning to combine your finances? Creating a budget is often the best place to start. How will you approach financial planning?

INVESTMENTS

1. How do you feel about investing our money together?

2. What kind of investments are you most comfortable with?

3. Do you have existing investments?

GETTING FINANCIAL ADVICE

1. Are you open to working with a financial planner?

2. Who do you go to for financial advice?

3. What's the best financial advice you've been given?

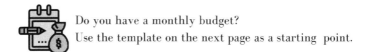 Do you have a monthly budget?
Use the template on the next page as a starting point.

Monthly
BUDGET

Month:

ITEM	BUDGET	SPENT	PLAN	REMAINS

TOTAL:

ITEM	BUDGET	SPENT	PLAN	REMAINS

TOTAL:

ITEM	BUDGET	SPENT	PLAN	REMAINS

TOTAL:

Monthly BUDGET

Month:

ITEM	BUDGET	SPENT	PLAN	REMAINS

TOTAL:

ITEM	BUDGET	SPENT	PLAN	REMAINS

TOTAL:

ITEM	BUDGET	SPENT	PLAN	REMAINS

TOTAL:

Monthly
BUDGET

Month:

ITEM	BUDGET	SPENT	PLAN	REMAINS

TOTAL:

ITEM	BUDGET	SPENT	PLAN	REMAINS

TOTAL:

ITEM	BUDGET	SPENT	PLAN	REMAINS

TOTAL:

Monthly BUDGET

Month:

ITEM	BUDGET	SPENT	PLAN	REMAINS

TOTAL:

ITEM	BUDGET	SPENT	PLAN	REMAINS

TOTAL:

ITEM	BUDGET	SPENT	PLAN	REMAINS

TOTAL:

Monthly
BUDGET

Month:

ITEM	BUDGET	SPENT	PLAN	REMAINS

TOTAL:

ITEM	BUDGET	SPENT	PLAN	REMAINS

TOTAL:

ITEM	BUDGET	SPENT	PLAN	REMAINS

TOTAL:

Monthly BUDGET

Month:

ITEM	BUDGET	SPENT	PLAN	REMAINS

TOTAL:

ITEM	BUDGET	SPENT	PLAN	REMAINS

TOTAL:

ITEM	BUDGET	SPENT	PLAN	REMAINS

TOTAL:

WHAT IFS

NAVIGATING THROUGH CHALLENGING TIMES

WHAT IF...?
If things don't go to plan

Two people get into a relationship as a commitment to each other. No one plans to breakup let alone file for divorce. But circumstances and people can change. It's not fun to plan for the worse-case scenario but if it might be necessary. Perhaps divorce isn't part of your values or it's not an option for either or both of you. This is a good time to explore the 'what ifs'.

THOUGHTS ABOUT DIVORCE AND BREAKING UP

1. Do you believe two people should breakup/file for divorce?

2. If so, how will we know it's time to end a relationship?

3. What are some things we could do to repair our relationship?

THE LOGISTICS

1. Who would move out of the house? (Is cohabitation an option?)

2. Would we hire attorneys to manage the process or can it be resolved on our own?

3. How would we divide our finances?

NOTES

_____   _____

_____   _____

_____   _____

_____   _____

WHAT IF...?

If things don't go to plan and you have a family together

Breakups are tough no matter your age, circumstance or how long you have been together. It's even more challenging when you have a family together. Everyone deals with breakups differently but when you have dependents, it's even more important that you agree on an approach to help your family cope with the changes. Use this page to reflect.

TIME WITH FAMILY

1. If kids or children are involved, how would we organise their time with each of us?

2. How could we make this transition as smooth as possible for them?

3. How could we still spend time as a family while being apart?

NOTES/THINGS TO ACTION

_____   _____

_____   _____

_____   _____

_____   _____

_____   _____

_____   _____

_____   _____

WAYS TO RECONNECT WHEN OUR RELATIONSHIP IS CHALLENGING

DATE EACH OTHER AGAIN

Remember when you first met? Re-create those dates you went on.

TAKE NOTES

Ask your partner how their day was, and really listen.

SURPRISE EACH OTHER

Nothing says 'I Love You' like a thoughtful gesture or a treat. Think of ways you can let your partner know that he/she is special. .

GET PROFESSIONAL HELP

If you feel like you've tried everything and nothing is improving your relationship, seek the help of a professional who can give you an objective point of view.

CHANGE IT UP

It's easy for a relationship to fall into a rut. Break out of the routine and do something different. For example, instead of having dinner on the couch, go out instead or order takeaway and have a candle light dinner.

INSERT YOUR IDEAS HERE

INSERT YOUR IDEAS HERE

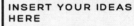

WRITE A LETTER

If you have trouble expressing how you feel, put it in a love letter.

THE ROMANCE PLAN

Using the following pages to map out your plan for romance. The first one is filled to give you an example.

Date:

Theme: The great outdoors

Activity: A hike in the Blue Mountains followed by a pinic

Itinerary i.e. how many hours will you need

1. Leave the house at 8am and drive to Katoomba Falls
2. Hike from Katoomba Falls to Three Sisters
3. Set up a lunch picnic

Materials Needed:

1. Sunscreen
2. Hiking Shoes
3. Picnic

What Needs to Be Organised?

1. Lunch
2. Transportation/public transport?

What are some things we can do to spark a little romance?

- Set up a playlist of our favourite songs of all time

- Stay and watch the sunset

- Go for a swim together

- Feed each other lunch

How did It go?

It was fun to break out of our usual routine. Though we didn't get a chance to talk about the issues going on, it was probably a good idea to take a break from it.

THE ROMANCE PLAN

Using the following pages to map out your plan for romance.

Date:

Theme:

Activity:

Itinerary i.e. how many hours will you need

Materials Needed:

What Needs to Be Organised?

What are some things we can do to spark a little romance?

How did It go?

THE ROMANCE PLAN

Using the following pages to map out your plan for romance.

Date:

Theme:

Activity:

Itinerary i.e. how many hours will you need

Materials Needed:

What Needs to Be Organised?

What are some things we can do to spark a little romance?

How did It go?

THE ROMANCE PLAN

Using the following pages to map out your plan for romance.

Date:

Theme:

Activity:

Itinerary i.e. how many hours will you need

Materials Needed:

What Needs to Be Organised?

What are some things we can do to spark a little romance?

How did It go?

THE ROMANCE PLAN

Using the following pages to map out your plan for romance.

Date:

Theme:

Activity:

Itinerary i.e. how many hours will you need

Materials Needed:

What Needs to Be Organised?

What are some things we can do to spark a little romance?

How did It go?

THE ROMANCE PLAN

Using the following pages to map out your plan for romance.

Date:

Theme:

Activity:

Itinerary i.e. how many hours will you need

Materials Needed:

What Needs to Be Organised?

What are some things we can do to spark a little romance?

How did It go?

THE ROMANCE PLAN

Using the following pages to map out your plan for romance.

Date:

Theme:

Activity:

Itinerary i.e. how many hours will you need

Materials Needed:

What Needs to Be Organised?

What are some things we can do to spark a little romance?

How did It go?

Ways to Strengthen our Relationship

PREPARE IN ADVANCE

If you expect to teach remotely in the near future, look at the curriculum in advance and prepare lessons for the weeks ahead.

Opt for content that's easily accessible online, in a variety of mediums.

SCHEDULE STUDENT CHECK-IN TIMES

Set time when you and your students can touch base and have them prepare questions they had during the exercises.

Make use of video conference tools that allow for multiple people to dial in.

SET UP A WORK ZONE

Set up a comfortable, well-lit area and designate it for work.

Avoid working from the couch or bed - when it is time to relax your brain might find it hard to shut off work thoughts.

CREATE AN ONLINE QUIZ

Check in on your students' learning progress through online methods.

Use a tool like Google Forms to make an online quiz any student can fill out with their device.

OVER-COMMUNICATE

Set out your expectations clearly in all relevant communication channels.

Make sure students know exactly where to receive their assignments, submit their work, or ask questions.

BE FLEXIBLE

Be empathetic of the home situation of students as some may not have available adult supervision or reliable internet.

If students need special support, be open to their unique needs.

HOW WOULD YOU DESCRIBE US?

Let's take a break from conversations. Circle the first word you see in this word search

S	U	N	L	A	N	F	U	N
U	S	T	O	X	I	C	L	N
N	H	T	V	W	C	L	S	O
B	E	N	I	U	E	A	A	R
L	L	W	N	R	D	I	N	M
O	R	O	C	K	Y	S	R	A
H	E	A	L	T	H	Y	H	D
K	U	W	A	V	E	S	C	N
W	O	N	D	E	R	F	U	L

WHAT WORDS DID YOU FIND?

THE FIGHT PLAN

MANAGING HEALTHY CONFLICT

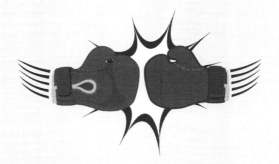

MANAGING CONFLICT

How to best manage conflict

Conflict is part and parcel in a relationship. In fact, most experts will agree that it is healthy in a relationship as long as it's approached in a constructive way. Everyone has different ways of dealing with conflict. Some are avoidant and would rather bury issues under a rug while others might need to resolve conflict as soon as it arises.

In our marriage, my husband and I have completely different styles of dealing with conflict. It's taken us awhile to come up with a happy medium that works for the both of us. Use these questions as a guide to come up with your own fight plan.

HANDLING CONFLICT

1. Which of the following conflict styles best describe you?

High

Assertiveness

Dominate
- High conflict
- Moderate stress

Collaborate
- Low conflict
- Low stress

Avoid
- High conflict
- High stress

Accomodate
- Low conflict
- Moderate stress

Low

High

Cooperativeness

Understanding your triggers

It's important to understand what makes you and your partner tick. What irritates you? It could be something as simple as: "I feel triggered when my partner raises his/her voice or walks away from a heated conversation".

TRIGGER 1:

_____
_____
_____
_____

TRIGGER 2:

_____
_____
_____
_____

TRIGGER 3:

_____
_____
_____

Understanding your triggers

It's important to understand what makes you and your partner tick. What irritates you? It could be something as simple as: "I feel triggered when my partner raises his/her voice or walks away from a heated conversation".

TRIGGER 1:

_____
_____
_____
_____

TRIGGER 2:

_____
_____
_____
_____

TRIGGER 3:

_____
_____
_____
_____

The Fight Plan
NAVIGATING CONFLICT TOGETHER

PARTNER A:
When you are involved in a heated discussion of conflict, what do you need from your partner?

PARTNER B:
When you are involved in a heated discussion of conflict, what do you need from your partner?

PARTNER A:
When conflict escalates, what do you need to cope with the stress?

PARTNER B:
When conflict escalates, what do you need to cope with the stress?

THREE THINGS WE'LL DO WHEN THINGS GET HEATED

CONFLICT RESOLUTION

Breakdown your conflict to get to the root of your problem

HOW DID THE CONFLICT START?

DID THE CONFLICT ESCALATE? WHAT TRIGGERED IT?

HOW DID YOU BOTH FEEL?

CAN YOU THINK ABOUT THE ROOT CAUSE OF THE CONFLICT?

WHAT DID YOU LEARN FROM IT? HOW COULD YOU BOTH DO BETTER?

TOOLS TO HELP YOU MANAGE EVERYDAY STRESS

Organise the everyday

Use the following tools to get your life organised and reduce the stress in your lives.

MEAL PLANNING

When you're both working during the week. thinking about dinner ideas can be overwhelming and take away the time you could have spent with each other. Plan ahead.

MON

AM
NN
PM

TUES

AM
NN
PM

WED

AM
NN
PM

THU

AM
NN
PM

FRI

AM
NN
PM

SAT

AM
NN
PM

SUN

AM
NN
PM

THINGS TO BUY

NOTES:

MEAL PLANNING

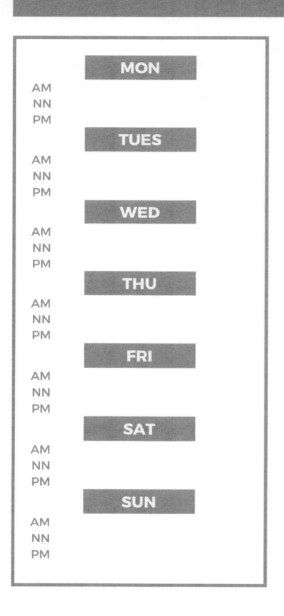

MON

AM
NN
PM

TUES

AM
NN
PM

WED

AM
NN
PM

THU

AM
NN
PM

FRI

AM
NN
PM

SAT

AM
NN
PM

SUN

AM
NN
PM

THINGS TO BUY

NOTES:

MEAL PLANNING

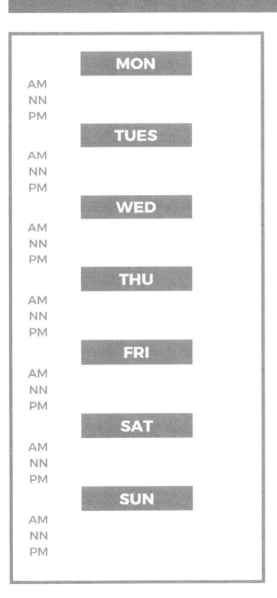

MON

AM
NN
PM

TUES

AM
NN
PM

WED

AM
NN
PM

THU

AM
NN
PM

FRI

AM
NN
PM

SAT

AM
NN
PM

SUN

AM
NN
PM

THINGS TO BUY

NOTES:

MEAL PLANNING

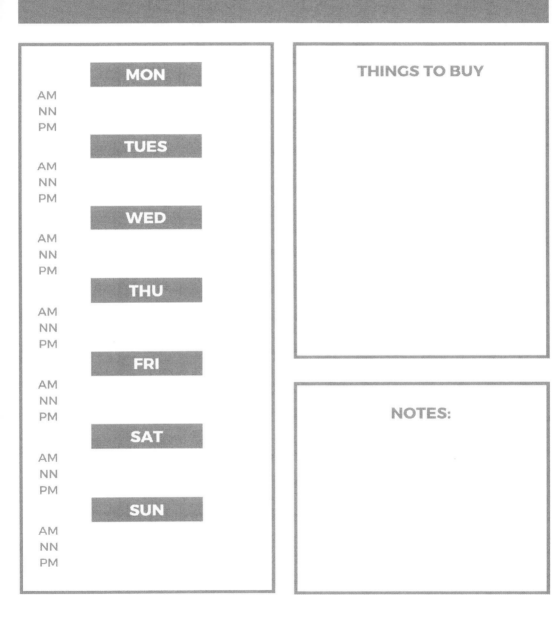

MON

AM
NN
PM

TUES

AM
NN
PM

WED

AM
NN
PM

THU

AM
NN
PM

FRI

AM
NN
PM

SAT

AM
NN
PM

SUN

AM
NN
PM

THINGS TO BUY

NOTES:

Our Weekly Cleaning List

Most arguments stem from unresolved issues and you may find that household chores are one of them. If you're living together, work out what each person is responsible for.

ASSIGNED TASKS	FAMILY MEMBER NUMBER 1	FAMILY MEMBER NUMBER 2	FAMILY MEMBER NUMBER 3	FAMILY MEMBER NUMBER 4
BEDROOM				
LIVING ROOM				
BATHROOM 1				
BATHROOM 2				
KITCHEN				
GARDEN				
PLAY ROOM				
LAUNDRY				

STARTING A FAMILY

ALIGNING WANTS AND NEEDS

STARTING A FAMILY

Aligning what both partners need

Starting a family is a big step in a relationship. And not every couple may agree on an approach. Having children is a lifetime commitment and both people need to be working towards the same timeline. You might find that by having these
discussions, your relationship may take another turn.

No matter how big or
intimidating this topic may be, it's best to have it sooner rather than later. I've witnessed many scenarios where a couple has dated for 3+ years and when they finally have the talk about starting a family, it's revealed that one a person doesn't want to have children.

Once you decide if a family is in the cards, you'll then want to decide how to approach it. Trying to conceive can be a stressful process. Use the next set of questions as your guide.

STARTING A FAMILY

1. Do you want children?

2. How many children would you like to have?

3. Would you be open to adoption?

PREPARING FOR A FAMILY

1. What do you think we need to do to prepare for a family?

2. What are some signs that we are ready?

3. Would you be open to doing a full health check?

STARTING A FAMILY

Are you ready to start a family?

Every couple has their own timeline when it comes to starting a family. "So when are you guys going to have babies?" may be an easy question to dodge but if you don't have the answer, it might be time to start the discussion.

READY FOR CHANGE

1. Imagine a life where a little human will be dependent on you. How do you feel about that?

2. Do you feel pressured to have kids because of family or your age?

3. Have you achieved everything you wanted to? If not, can you put your goals/needs on hold?

ALL ABOUT TIMING

1. What is a good age to start a family?

2. Are we in a good financial position to start a family?

3. If we accidentally fell pregnant, how would you feel?

STARTING A FAMILY

Trying to Conceive

Planning for a family is a big step but even when you have a plan in place, it doesn't always go the way you want it to. If you are talking about starting a family, you might want to consider what would happen if it takes longer to fall pregnant.

TRYING TO CONCEIVE

1. How would you want to approach trying to conceive?

2. Would you be open to IVF and fertility treatments?

3. Are you prepared to invest in treatments to help us conceive?

NOTES/THINGS TO ACTION

_____   _____
_____   _____
_____   _____
_____   _____
_____   _____
_____   _____
_____   _____

HOW I FEEL ABOUT STARTING A FAMILY NOW PARTNER A:

In these clouds, write down all of your thoughts and feelings you have about starting a family.

Fold along the dotted line so the two stars touch.

HOW I FEEL ABOUT STARTING A FAMILY NOW PARTNER B:

In these clouds, write down all of your thoughts and feelings you have about starting a family.

Fold along the dotted line so the two stars touch.

WORK/LIFE BALANCE

HOW MUCH DO YOU NEED?

WORK/LIFE BALANCE
Setting time aside for you

Work life balance can be a hefty goal to achieve. Do you and your partner have the same standards when it comes to work/life balance? Often in our 30s and 40s, work/life balance can take a backseat. Take the time to see if you're carving out the time you both need to reset as individuals and as a couple.

WORK/LIFE BALANCE

1. How do you define work/life balance??

2. Are you happy with how much time you spend in front of your laptop working?

3. Do you think your working hours affect ou relationship?

OUT OF OFFICE HOURS

1. What do you think about working outside office hours?

2. How do you feel about working on a weekend??

3. How would you feel about me working on a weekend?

WORK/LIFE BALANCE

Helping each other build a meaningful life

It's easy to let work consume your time if you have a demanding job. Make a pact to help each other stay on track with personal and life goals. You may enjoy your job but there may be other aspects of your life that need your attention too.

WHEN AN INTERVENTION IS NEEDED

1. What are some signs you might be burnt out from work?

2. How can I help you when work is really busy?

3. How firm do you want me to be when it comes to making sure you finish work on time?

4. What are some things I can do to make sure you have a healthy work/life balance?

5. How can we make sure we always find time for 'us'?

6. What helps you unwind after a long day of work?

7. When it comes to your career, what can I do to support you?

WEEKLY WORK SCHEDULE

NAME:

DATE:

MONDAY

TUESDAY

WEDNESDAY

THURSDAY

FRIDAY

WEEKLY WORK SCHEDULE

NAME:

DATE:

MONDAY

TUESDAY

WEDNESDAY

THURSDAY

FRIDAY

RELAX

REFRESH

RECHARGE

30 DAY WORK/LIFE CHALLENGE

Think of 30 ways you can carve some time out for your relationship. It could be something as quick and simple as a 30 second hug.

1	2	3	4	5
i.e. Cook breakfast together				
6	7	8	9	10
11	12	13	14	15
16	17	18	19	20
21	22	23	24	25
26	27	28	29	30

The Not To-Do List

STUFF THAT DISTRACTS ME

STUFF THAT GIVES ME ANXIETY

STUFF THAT DRAINS MY ENERGY

STUFF I FEEL OBLIGATED TODO

STUFF THAT ACTUALLY DOESN'T NEED TO BE DONE

STUFF I CAN'T CONTROL/AM NOT RESPONSIBLE FOR

MY TOP NOT TO DO THINGS

The Not To-Do List

STUFF THAT DISTRACTS ME

STUFF THAT GIVES ME ANXIETY

STUFF THAT DRAINS MY ENERGY

STUFF I FEEL OBLIGATED TODO

STUFF THAT ACTUALLY DOESN'T NEED TO BE DONE

STUFF I CAN'T CONTROL/AM NOT RESPONSIBLE FOR

MY TOP NOT TO DO THINGS

THE BACK UP PLAN

CAREER BREAKS AND LIFE'S TWISTS AND TURNS

CAREER BREAKS

Planning for the unexpected

Things don't always go to plan. One of you might lose your job, fall ill
or need a break from work. These events often cause strain in a relationship
without a fall-back plan.

How will you tackle these challenges together as a
couple? What plans will you put in place to minimise the strain a life setback
will cause?

CAREER BREAKS AND UNEMPLOYMENT

1. In 2020, we saw that our jobs are never a guarantee. What happens when one or both of us lose our jobs?

2. Do you agree that if one of us loses their job, the other should contribute more to household expenses?

3. How do you feel about us saving money for a rainy day?

4. How much do you think we should set aside for our rainy day fund?

5. Do you have business or unemployment insurance?

6. How would you feel if one of us wanted to take a career break?

7. Would you be interested in creating multiple streams of income?

GOOD HEALTH

In sickness and in health

No amount of money or time can buy you good health. How will you nurture your bodies so you're as healthy as possible both mentally and physically?

CHEERS TO GOOD HEALTH

1. On a scale of 1-10, 10 being the most healthy, how would you rate your health?

2. How would you describe your eating habits?

3. How well do you know your family's health history?

4. Do you have health insurance? If so, are you familiar with your level of coverage?

5. What would happen if one of us fell ill? i.e. Who would help us run our daily errands, help look after the family?

NOTES/THINGS TO ACTION

_____   _____

_____   _____

_____   _____

_____   _____

Ways to stay healthy

Think about 30 things you can do to maintain good health

STAYING
FULFILLED

INDEPENDENTLY AND TOGETHER

WHAT MAKES YOU HAPPY
Independence and 'me time'

'Me time' gives couples a chance to indulge in their passions and gain independence from a relationship. When a couple has been together for a long time, it's easy to lose their independence. It's easy to fall into the trap of mediocre. I always want to be the type of person my husband fell in love with. And now that our family is growing, it's even more important that we take time to nurture ourselves.

YOUR MUST DOS

1. When you've had a rough week, what replenishes you?

2. Where is your happy place and how often do you need to go there?

3. How much 'me time' do you need a week?

4. If I needed more 'me time' than you did, would you be fine with it?

5. What are some things you love to do and you'll always want to do?

NOTES/THINGS TO ACTION

_____   _____

_____   _____

_____   _____

_____   _____

self-care check-in

CHECK THE BOXES OF THE ACTIVITIES YOU DO TO TAKE CARE OF YOURSELF.

- [ ] EAT THREE HEALTHY MEALS
- [ ] TAKE A BREAK FROM SOCIAL MEDIA ALL DAY
- [ ] FIND A QUIET SPOT TO MEDITATE
- [ ] FOUND TIME FOR AROMATHERAPY
- [ ] DO A GRATITUDE LIST
- [ ] PRACTICE DEEP BREATHING
- [ ] LISTEN TO GOOD MUSIC
- [ ] EXERCISE
- [ ] CATCH UP WITH A FRIEND
- [ ] VISIT A FAMILY MEMBER
- [ ] SPEND TIME OUTDOORS
- [ ] HAVE A MINI PAMPER SESH
- [ ] CUDDLE A PET
- [ ] TRY SOMETHING NEW
- [ ] READ A BOOK

SELF-CARE
Bingo

TOOK A SHOWER	ATE A HEALTHY MEAL	CAUGHT UP WITH FRIENDS	PROCESSED MY FEELINGS	COMPLIMENTED MYSELF
EXERCISED	MEDITATED	COOKED A HEALTHY SNACK	PLAYED WITH MY PET	DID A SHEET MASK
TOOK A BREAK	DRANK WATER	Free	TOOK A SOCIAL MEDIA BREAK	TREATED MYSELF
COMPLIMENTED SOMEONE	GOT 8 HOURS OF SLEEP	TAMED NEGATIVE THOUGHTS	HUGGED SOMEONE	DROPPED A HABIT
TOOK A MENTAL HEALTH DAY	SPENT TIME WITH NATURE	DECLUTTERED MY SPACE	WROTE IN MY JOURNAL	PRACTICED COMPASSION

Starting an Attitude of Gratitude

I'm grateful for...

the gift of family	my dog	my health and well-being	blessings to share with others	the freedom to be my true self
simple joys that lift me up	people who remain in my life	food on the table	peace of mind	my siblings
my grand-parents	the opportunity to learn from mistakes	*Free*	the stars in the sky	wisdom to know what's right from what's wrong
a chance to begin again	the roof over my head	internet connection	receiving forgiveness	my cat
encouraging words from my support system	the kindness of strangers	freedom of speech	rainbows after the storm	my best friends

FUN STUFF

Now that you've made it through all seven conversations, it's time to take a break and have some fun.

WE JUST FIT.

get to know me

cat	dog
chicken	duck
llama	sloth
rabbit	guinea pig
snake	spider
turtle	fish
mouse	hedgehog
lion	tiger
giraffe	zebra

How to play: Circle the answer you
think your partner would pick.

get to know me

cat	dog
chicken	duck
llama	sloth
rabbit	guinea pig
snake	spider
turtle	fish
mouse	hedgehog
lion	tiger
giraffe	zebra

How to play: Circle the answer you
think your partner would pick.

THIS OR THAT

Make Your Own Birthday Dessert

Cake	Cheesecake
Red velvet	S'mores
Sprinkles	Fruit toppings
Buttercream	Cream cheese
Apple pie	Turtle pie
Lemon bars	Fudge brownies
Chocolate chip	Oatmeal
Milkshake	Gelato
Strawberry	Lemon
Cinnamon rolls	Tarts

THIS OR THAT

Make Your Own Birthday Dessert

Cake	Cheesecake
Red velvet	S'mores
Sprinkles	Fruit toppings
Buttercream	Cream cheese
Apple pie	Turtle pie
Lemon bars	Fudge brownies
Chocolate chip	Oatmeal
Milkshake	Gelato
Strawberry	Lemon
Cinnamon rolls	Tarts

THE WORK EDITION

THIS OR THAT

FACE TO FACE	REMOTE MEET
LUNCH SOCIALS	AFTER WORK COCKTAILS
PHYSICAL NOTES	ONLINE DOCS
SCREEN SHARING	WHITEBOARD + MARKER
STICKY NOTES	ONLINE COLLAB APPS
OFFICE PLANTS	OFFICE PETS
CASUAL FRIDAYS	NO DRESS CODE

THIS OR THAT

THIS	THAT
FACE TO FACE	REMOTE MEET
LUNCH SOCIALS	AFTER WORK COCKTAILS
PHYSICAL NOTES	ONLINE DOCS
SCREEN SHARING	WHITEBOARD + MARKER
STICKY NOTES	ONLINE COLLAB APPS
OFFICE PLANTS	OFFICE PETS
CASUAL FRIDAYS	NO DRESS CODE

THE END

OTHER BOOKS YOU MIGHT LIKE

Notes

Notes

Notes

Notes